# Penzance and Newlyn

## IN OLD PHOTOGRAPHS

# Penzance
# and Newlyn

## IN OLD PHOTOGRAPHS

*Collected by*
JONATHAN HOLMES

Alan Sutton Publishing Limited
Phoenix Mill · Far Thrupp
Stroud · Gloucestershire

First published 1992

Copyright © Jonathan Holmes 1992

British Library Cataloguing
in Publication Data

Holmes, Jonathan
  Penzance and Newlyn in Old Photographs
  I. Title
  942.37

  ISBN 0-7509-0212-4

Typeset in 9/10 Sabon.
Typesetting and origination by
Alan Sutton Publishing Limited.
Printed and bound by
WBC, Bridgend, Mid Glam.

# Contents

# Introduction

The aim of this book is to show the diversity of life that characterizes the Penzance area past and present, from the busy fishing industry to the thriving artistic community. The photographs are mainly from the collections housed at Penzance and District Museum, with a small number from the Penzance (subscription) Library and the Local Studies Library in Redruth.

Any book of photographs must include people. They make and shape history. We all know that history can be illustrated through artefacts but it is the people who used them that matter. The tools owned by the wheelwright and the mangle used by the housewife tell their own story, while the clothes they wear illustrate their status in the community, but these things are interesting because they tell us something about their owners' daily lives.

Many of the photographs show that there have been major changes to trade in Penzance. One hundred years ago the town centre was a markedly different place: with no chain stores there was a diverse range of individual businesses including grocers, ironmongers, photographers and butchers, as well as the many palaces of refreshment – public houses. Market-day saw the streets throng with people from the whole Penwith area. Penzance had a number of markets, from the fish market just off New Street that was demolished to make way for the telephone exchange, to the Shambles meat market. The main Market House with its impressive dome is now the home of Lloyds Bank.

Entertainment is a part of everyday life and can range from a visit to the cinema or theatre to taking part in a street festival. The area at one time had four cinemas: the Savoy, the Gaiety, the Regal and the Ritz. Today only the Savoy survives. The Pavilion Theatre has long since ceased trading and the town now only offers the open air theatre in Penlee Park and the Acorn in Parade Street. The re-launching of The Feast of St John, Mazey Day, should be welcomed, and generally it has been well received. The mysterious serpent dance has been reintroduced but the tar-barrels and bonfines have been wisely forgotten.

The area has three harbours, at Mousehole, Newlyn and Penzance. Those at Newlyn and Mousehole pre-date that at Penzance by many hundreds of years. Mousehole is no longer a working harbour but Newlyn Harbour has grown from strength to strength. The extensions of Newlyn Harbour and the new fish market have changed this quaint area for ever. The busy harbour at Penzance is the staging post for the Isles of Scilly, offering a regular steamer passenger service as well as a recently introduced cargo service. The dry dock, under the management of N. Holmans and Sons, sees many a vessel skilfully negotiating the narrow entrance once the Ross Bridge has been swung out of the way.

The town was cut off from the outside world, with access only by a rough road and the sea, until the railway arrived in 1852. The age of the train had come. Soon the link across the Tamar meant that the area's produce could be shipped to London. Of course the benefits were not only one way: the fast expresses that tore down from London and other parts of the country brought the town a new industry, tourism. Until the advent of the motor coach in the 1930s and the rise of ownership of the motor car in the 1950s, nearly everyone came to Cornwall by train. The 'Cornish Riviera', 'The Cornishman' and 'The Flying Dutchman' were but a few. Today it seems that the motor car has come to stay.

Newlyn has become internationally famous, not for its fish but for its artistic community. Although artists had visited for centuries, it was not until 1882 that the first artist to be associated with the Newlyn School settled in the area. His name was Walter Langley, a young Birmingham artist, a socialist who had great empathy for the people of Newlyn. His famous paintings, *Oh for a touch of a vanished hand, and the sound of a voice that is stilled*, *Breadwinners* and *Disaster,* all depict the life of the village's inhabitants. The artists of the Newlyn School included Stanhope Forbes, Elizabeth Forbes (neé Armstrong), Edwin Harris, Norman Garstin and Ralph Todd. A later group included Harold Knight, Laura Knight, Dod Procter, Ernest Procter, Alfred Munnings and Lamorna Birch. Today the Penwith area has the largest artistic community in Europe. Contemporary art is regularly displayed at the Newlyn Art Gallery which was set up by the philanthropist Passmore Edwards.

The area has had a variety of industries, mining being the most famous; the ores extracted included copper and tin, and china clay (kaolin) was first discovered at Godolphin by Cookworthy. Clay pits existed on the St Just road and towards St Ives. The quarries from Castle an Dinas to Penlee and Lamorna have provided aggregate and granite for the roads and buildings of the area. Agriculture and horticulture remain major industries, their wares being sold at the weekly market in Penzance. Today the spread of business workshops from Chyandour to Eastern Green and beyond has altered the entrance into the town. These workshops and Finns shoe factory provide important employment in addition to that offered by the seasonal tourist industry.

Jonathan J. Holmes
Curator of the Penzance and District Museum and Art Gallery

# SECTION ONE

# People

Penzance Board of Guardians, 25 April 1889. This stalwart group was responsible for the running of Madron Workhouse, which was built in 1839 and had the dubious accolade of spending the least amount of money per inmate.

Carte-de-visite, by the famous Penzance photographer John Gibson, whose studios were on the Terrace in Market Jew Street. These small portrait photographs became popular from 1850.

Carte-de-visite, by J. Moody. This lesser-known photographer had studios in Penzance and Redruth. Both of the carte-de-visites in this volume were presented to Penzance Museum by descendants of the Quick family (see p. 14).

Cabinet card, by Robert H. Preston, who was granted a royal warrant as a result of his photographs of the visit of the Prince and Princess of Wales to Botallack Mine on 25 July 1865.

J.T. Blight, author, engraver, and artist. Born in 1837, his most famous book, *A Week at the Lands End*, about travelling in the far west of Cornwall, was first published in 1861. He died in 1901.

Elizabeth and John Richards Branwell at the waterspout by the pond at the Trewithen Road entrance to their estate, now Penlee Park. The family owned a large mill at Gulval. Their offices and storage facilities were opposite the railway station, now erroneously named Branwell Mill.

John Branwell, eldest son of Elizabeth and J.R. Branwell. He was virtually disinherited by his parents when he wished to marry Elizabeth Pollard, the daughter of a Penzance shopkeeper. He was a talented amateur photographer.

Penzance Rifle Volunteers. Back row, left to right: ? Goddard, ? Tanrock, J. Paul, W. Caldwell, ? Jenkins, ? Stewart. Front row: W. Motton, W. Stevens, Col ? Coldwell, ? Warren, -?-. Front centre: Sergeant-Major ? Sainsbury.

The Quick family, c. 1915. Standing, left to right: Annie Quick, James Stoate, Elsie Quick. Seated: James Quick and his wife. Centre: James Stoate, who was born in 1910.

Spargo wedding group, 11 October 1930. Back row, left to right: Joseph Rowe, William Polgrean jun. Front row: Grace Harvey, Berenice Llewellyn, Lionel Spargo, Margaret Spargo (née Polgrean), Marie Thomas, Margaret Polgrean, William Polgrean. All the women are wearing dresses made and designed by Margaret Spargo using Cryséde hand-printed silk which was manufactured at Sambos Row in Newlyn.

William Henry Prowse. Born in Paul in 1884, he was a stonemason by trade and a keen amateur racing cyclist in his spare time. He is said to have ridden his bike from the bottom of Paul Hill to Chywoone in just three minutes. In the early 1900s he was the Devon and Cornwall Cycle Champion. He died in 1967.

Heamoor United cup team, 1908–9. Back row, left to right: Warren, Nicholson, Trevennen, Jenkin, Baker, Harris, Penpraze. Front row: Eustace, Nicholson, Stevens (capt.), Cocks. Top right: J.T. Tresize, trainer.

St John's Boys National School, 1904. This school was situated in Queen Street and opened in 1872. Penzance gained full parish status in 1871 so that the vicar could legally become a trustee of this school.

Visit of the Lord Mayor of London, 2 June 1909. The Mayor of Penzance welcomes him on the steps of the Public Buildings, known today as St John's Hall.

Old Davey, the watercress seller, in Cornwall Terrace. Such sellers, hawkers and pedlars were common in and around West Cornwall in the late 1880s and early 1900s.

Phyllis Rowe, Penzance water carrier, *c.* 1880. She filled her jugs at the well in Wellfields and charged 2d. per pitcher.

Fire-tender behind St John's Hall during the Second World War. These small tenders could be towed to the site of a fire and were used as auxilliary machines throughout the war.

Penzance Boys Grammar School staff, *c*. 1950. Standing, left to right: Elevet Thomas, Ben Batten, E. Tarbet, E. Guard, H. Harvey, J. Pascoe, Jim Batten, D. Waller, J. Munroe, M. Hogg, Frank Murray, ? Stewart, Fred Jarvis, Stan Jarris. Seated: D. MacCarthy, Mrs Biddle (secretary), A. Tregenza, J. Wightman, W. Williams, T.C. Rising (headmaster), D. Jones, H. Otto, Mrs R. Sibson, T. Petters and Donald Behenna.

Penzance Health and Strength Club members give a gymnastic display outside the Boys Grammar School.

Penzance Borough Council, 1932. Mayor Alderman R. Hall, Town Clerk E.W.J. Nicholson, Mace Bearers J. Matthews and T. Webber, Chief Constable H. Kenyon.

The last Penzance Borough Council, 1973–4. Mayor David Pooley, Town Clerk E.O. Wheale, Mace Bearers A. Fowler, C. James. Back, left: Le Yeoman Mr Desmond Mennear, who retired in 1992 after thirty-two years in office.

Mayor of Penzance, Alderman Alfred Beckerleg. He was mayor on three occasions, 1964, 1965 and 1966, and was granted the freedom of the town on 9 May 1988. He died in 1991.

Alverton estate is opened in 1954 by HRH Princess Mary, accompanied by the Mayor of Penzance, George Ford.

Beating the bounds. Mayor Mrs Lillian Garstin having her head touched on one of the Penzance Borough boundary stones on 8 May 1964. This was part of the celebrations marking the 350th anniversary of the granting of Penzance's charter.

# SECTION TWO

# Streets, Buildings and Parks

Market House, Penzance. The presence of the balcony on the Star Inn, which was removed in 1860, means that this is one of the earliest photographs of Penzance. The long exposure required at this time necessitated no movement to produce a clear photographic

Alverton Street, 1908. On the right is the First and Last Inn, the staging post for the horse-drawn buses which ran to all parts of West Cornwall.

Alverton Street, pre-1914. The railings on the left are the frontage to the home of photographer Robert Preston, while the Alverne Inn is on the right.

Market House from the west end, prior to its rebuilding. Constructed between 1836 and 1838, the symmetry of the original design was destroyed in the rebuilding.

Market House, 1922, being rebuilt in its present format with a rounded, somewhat art deco, west end. The bank opened in 1925.

Market stalls, Market Place, Penzance. On market-day and at weekends, stalls were set up alongside the Market House. This photograph dates from the 1930s and may remind readers of the paintings by Stanhope Forbes showing a similar view.

Old town reservoir, Causewayhead, Penzance. Later it was covered and became the site of the former cattle market which is today a car park. The reservoir supplied water to the various shoots in the town, and still feeds the fountain in Morrab Gardens.

The Market Cross is one of only two crosses in the area that bear inscriptions to Cornish kings. Originally sited in the Greenmarket, now outside Penzance Museum, the inscription reads REGIS RICATI CRUX, the Cross of King Ricatus. There are also other inscriptions including little figures. The cross is believed to date from between AD 900 and AD 930.

The west side of Queen Street, 1969, showing cottages just prior to their demolition. This is now the site of Chirgwin Court.

Causewayhead, Penzance, c. 1880. The leat in the left gutter was fed from the town reservoir at the top of the street.

St Anthony Cottages. The building on the left was the site of the Yacht Inn before it moved to Green Street and finally to its present position behind St Anthony's Gardens.

Deep in conversation. Many such buildings, with a vine or creeper growing up the cottage wall, could be found in Newlyn and Mousehole.

The Fradgan, Jenny Lind Court, named after the boat in the centre of the picture. Note the capstan. This little courtyard was popular with photographers for its variety of views.

The Coombe, Newlyn, 1908. The granite buildings on the left were built as fish stores, while among the trees on the right is the vicarage.

The palm avenue entrance to Morrab Gardens from Morrab Road, 1908. The house and grounds were purchased by the borough in 1888 for £3, 120.

Morrab Gardens, 1906. The bandstand was donated by J.H. Bennetts and opened on 4 August 1905.

Penzance Military Band, *c.* 1914. The bandstands in Morrab Gardens and on the Promenade were popular attractions, with evening and weekend concerts. The chairs on the far right are still used by Penwith District Council and Penzance Town Council.

Hydrangeas in bloom, November 1925. This photograph was taken for a tourist guidebook extolling the virtues of the Cornish Riviera's climate.

Cornish Shakespearean Festival, held yearly in Penlee Park in the 1950s. When this theatre opened, the Minack Open Air Theatre at Porthcurno was still in its infancy.

Penlee Park Open Air Theatre, c. 1950. A Shakespearean play is being performed. The theatre ceased to be used in the early 1960s and it was not until the late 1980s, when Penzance Town Council took over the running of the park, that a summer season was reintroduced.

Penlee Park, tennis tournament, c. 1950. The present club house had yet to be built. The grassed areas were terraced to provide seating.

The opening of the Rotary Club boating pool by Alderman Miss A.O. Chirgwin, Mayor of Penzance, on 5 August 1955. This pool was a great attraction, with model-yacht racing becoming a regular event.

Bedford Bolitho Gardens, looking east. These gardens were built on the site of the former Serpentine Factory. When the factory closed Mr Bedford Bolitho purchased the site and built an Italian Garden for the people of the town to enjoy.

Bedford Bolitho Gardens. The gardens were totally destroyed on the nights of 6 and 7 March 1962 by one of the most severe storms in living memory. Today it is the site of the Wherry Town car park and a children's play area.

# SECTION THREE

# Shops, Public Houses, Churches and Hotels

Causewayhead, *c.* 1895. At one time this street was known as North Street. The Stewart family were ironmongers and plumbers. The kettle sign is typical of the sort of signs seen up until the end of the nineteenth century; they enabled those who could not read to know what the shop sold. The next shop displays a similar sign, a barber's pole, and these can still be seen.

The Greenmarket from the top of Branwell Stores, photographed by John Branwell in the 1890s. This wide space was later reduced by moving the frontages on the right hand side up into line with that of Polsue's.

The Greenmarket from the roof of the Market House. Compare this with the previous photograph. The neon sign advertising the Ritz cinema in Queen Street has long gone.

Shakerleys Corner, 1895, so called after Shakerleys the chemist. The royal coat of arms is not a royal warrant but an indication that postage stamps were available.

Market Place, 1895. The central building was known as Branwell's Corner and was the site of Branwell's Stores. The building with bow windows on the left was Chudleigh's Eating House.

Market Jew Street, pre-1883. The statue of Sir Humphry Davy was erected in 1872. The lower building on the left is the site of the present post office which was built in 1883.

Barclays Bank, Market Jew Street, 1934. The bank was rebuilt in 1963 when the granite façade was replaced by a steel and glass structure. The view also shows Gibson's studio.

The Cornish Bank, Queens Square, 1880. In this view the bank is under construction, being incorporated in 1879. Its shareholders included J.R. Branwell of Penlee. The building is now the home of the Co-op supermarket.

W.H. Carnes, Clarence Street, c. 1900. One of the very earliest talking machines, an Edison phonograph, is on display. The device in front of the grand piano is the forerunner of the pianola. This example is a Simplex.

Market Place and Queens Square. This rare postcard shows W.B. Michell the jeweller, whose signs are preserved in the museum, with the Globe Inn in the background. The bicycle with a rickshaw trailer is certainly an unusual mode of transport.

J. Morrish, 68 Chapel Street, Penzance. The itinerant street musicians give this photograph additional interest.

Penzance and District Industrial Co-operative opposite Jennings Street on the Terrace, dating from between 1930 and 1935. The Society had a number of other shops in the town including those in Queens Square.

Wilton & Nicholls Ironmongers, c. 1920. Many local inhabitants will remember this useful shop which seemed to stock almost everything.

Clarks and Bodilly, outfitters and grocers respectively, 1885. Today this is the site of Simpsons, one of the last family businesses in the town. Next door is the Shambles market.

What on earth are you doing man?
Why, J am painting my trousers another colour. J had them from Simpson & Cᵒ 10 years ago and can't wear them out

An advertising postcard extolling the virtues of shopping at Simpsons. It is postmarked 1906.

Madame Legg, Market Jew Street. This shop was situated at the bottom of the street and initially sold ladies' gowns.

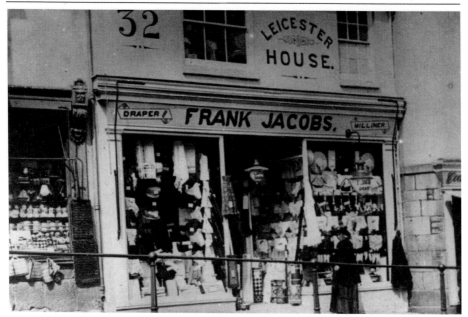

Frank Jacobs, Leicester House, *c.* 1890. The business in Market Jew Street opened in 1889 and, although sold in the 1920s, it remained trading until 1992 when it was forced into liquidation.

Frank Jacobs, known by many generations of West Cornwall families as outfitters, milliners and drapers, 1931. The slogan 'Everyone goes to Jacobs for hose' is similar to that on their original handcart, acquired by Penzance Museum at the liquidation sale, which reads, 'The Home of Drapery Economy'.

Advertising board, 1890. This tells a number of interesting stories. Israel Oppenheim's emporium sold furniture and musical instruments. He was a prominent member of a large Jewish community which existed in Penzance; the synagogue (Orthodox) in New Street closed in 1911. He and his wife are buried in the Jewish walled cemetery at Leskinnick. The Castle Line posters point to the large number of Cornish miners that had to emigrate to find employment, the gold mines in Natal being just one destination.

Shambles market. This meat market was dismantled in 1928. It had a right of way through it, which now runs up alongside Simpsons and into Bread Street.

The Three Tuns Hotel, Chyandour. This building, now demolished, stood on the open area to the right of the present horse trough.

Duke of Cumberland, Causewayhead, 1897. The occasion being celebrated was the Diamond Jubilee of Queen Victoria.

St Mary's chapel, a chapel of ease under the parish of Madron, seen here in an engraving by Vibert. The building was demolished in 1832 to make way for St Mary's church. The spire was a prominent feature of this chapel and was used as a local navigation mark.

Chapel Street and St Mary's church, 1903. The church was built in 1835. The house to the left of the tree was the childhood home of the mother and aunt of the Brontë sisters.

St Mary's church prior to its improvement under Canon Carr in the 1920s. The internationally famous artist Ernest Procter was commissioned to design a new reredos, which was in place until a disastrous fire on Saturday 23 March 1985.

St John's church, consecrated on 4 October 1881 by the Bishop of Truro, the Right Reverend Edward Benson DD. The cost of its construction was £6, 130.

St Peter's church, Newlyn, 1908. The building on the right is the church hall and Sunday school.

# SECTION FOUR

# Entertainments, Celebrations and Disasters

Corpus Christi fair, *c*. 1900. This annual fair was at one time a great occasion. In addition to the amusements it offered bioscopes, a forerunner of the cinema, and a circus. The elephants and horses were taken down to the harbour to bathe. The fairground ride on the left is a Razzle Dazzle, of which only one example still exists.

Corpus Christi fair, *c.* 1900. This view shows the side stalls, the Lighthouse Slip, and the bioscopes in the background. The bioscope shows attracted people into the tents where large mechanical organs from France accompanied girls who danced on the front stage.

Quay fair in the 1890s, part of the annual Midsummer Day festival that was held for centuries. By the late 1890s it had become only a pleasure fair. One nineteenth-century writer said of the festival, 'the streets would be ablaze with bonfires, tar-barrels, fireworks and torches, the people of the quay quarter would perform curious serpent dances, the whole bay would be ringed with fire.'

Early fairground bioscope show. This type of show was used before the advent of the larger, ornately carved showfronts of the late 1890s and early 1900s. The organ on the left hand side is a Trumpet Barrel organ, probably by Gavioli of Paris.

Pleasure fair, Tolcarne Bridge, Newlyn. This attraction, a type of cabaret theatre for the 1890s, was extremely popular with local inhabitants.

Opening programme of the Ritz, 27 July 1936. This palatial art deco cinema in Queens Street was part of the ABC network and was built for local inhabitants and tourists alike.

Ritz Compton cinema organ. This was the only installation of a cinema organ in Cornwall. The organ was a combination of a pipe organ and an electric organ called the Melotone. The console changed colour as the organist played.

The Hut, 9 August 1907. Prior to the building of the Pavilion, a tent or 'grand concert pavilion' was erected each season. Apart from its theatrical use, non-conformists held temperance meetings there.

The Pavilion, 1912. This theatre, roof tea-garden and palm-court dance-hall complex was a popular attraction. Today the building contains an amusement arcade and a restaurant.

War memorial on Battery Rocks. This was erected to the memory of all those from the borough who died in the First World War. It was unveiled on 14 May 1922.

War memorial, Newlyn. All communities, small and large, erected monuments to their dead following the First World War. The exact date of this photograph is unknown but it was obviously taken within a few years of the end of the war.

Welcome to the Royal Cornwall Agricultural Show, 1885. The show at this time travelled from town to town. Its arrival was a major occasion for any community and Penzance was no exception.

Chapel Street. The occasion is unknown but the sight of the Borough Police Force followed by the mayor, aldermen and councillors indicates that they are on their way to St Mary's church for a civic service.

Public Buildings during the First World War. A group of soldiers and their officers enter the forecourt of the buildings.

Public Buildings, photographed by Gibson. The occasion was obviously of some importance, as indicated by the Cavalry Troop in the courtyard and the men with their staves lining the road.

Leskinnick Terrace, *c.* 1920. The May horns on sale were blown by local children on May Day, usually early in the morning. This led to the town fathers banning their use. In defiance of this the late Cyril Orchard recounted that he used to stand outside the borough boundary to make his blowing legal.

Fleet review, 18 July 1910. The Royal Yacht progresses through the fleet of nearly two hundred British warships.

Western Union fleet, 1949. Mount's Bay was once again visited by a large fleet of 109 vessels. British, Dutch, French and Belgian warships were present.

Sailors and a few local girls hail the Western Union fleet. An open air dance was held on the promenade while a formal dance was hosted by the mayor in St John's Hall.

Road to Madron, 1891. This was the occasion of the great blizzard. The snow-drift towers over the heads of the youngsters.

Penlee estate, looking up the drive from the Trewithen Road entrance, 1891. The photographer was John Branwell.

Lannoweth Road during the Second World War. The bomb, which failed to explode, tore through the house, narrowly missing the occupants who were in bed.

Clearing the rubble. Emergency workers help to clear a way through bomb debris after an air raid.

Unexploded bomb. These children were extremely fortunate. Not long after this photograph was taken their school bell rang and they went inside. Minutes later the bomb exploded.

Mabbots Store during the Second World War. This building stood where the Shell Travellers Check service station is now sited.

Mabbots Store showing further bomb damage. Emergency workers help clear up while a policeman looks on.

'Bellair', the home of Dr W. Leslie, was bombed during the later part of 1940. It was never rebuilt and today the Ambulance Station and Health Clinic stand on the site.

Bottle-nosed whales, 1 July 1911. This school of nearly eighty whales stranded themselves on Eastern Green beach. Unfortunately, some people mutilated these mammals and eventually a marksman had to be called in to put them out of their misery.

The Promenade, looking east, showing the damage inflicted by a severe storm in 1880.
The building behind the main group is Nortons Baths which were demolished in 1883.

The Promenade, looking west, again depicting the damage caused by the storm of 1880.
The rubble strewn all over the road shows the severity of the occasion.

Alexandra Road, 1893. These cottages at the bottom of Alexandra Road were below the road level and here reveal the consequences of a flood.

The Promenade, Ash Wednesday storm, 1962. The damage caused by this storm was the worst in living memory, with the Promenade breached all along its length. The quick action of the Borough and County Councils ensured that the Promenade reopened in time for the 1962 season.

Cornwall Terrace, Ash Wednesday, 1962. The waves broke over the promenade and flooded Alexandra Road, Cornwall Terrace and Morrab Road.

Newlyn, 1962. The strength of the storm and the sea's swell is clearly shown here. Similar damage occurred in Newlyn in December 1989 and January 1990, and it is only in 1992 that a breakwater has been built at the entrance to the Newlyn River.

# SECTION FIVE

# Harbours

The paddle steamer SS *Galatea*, photographed by John Branwell in Penzance Harbour.

The premises in Penzance Harbour of James and John Burt: 'Ship & General Smithery Done Here, Block & Mast Maker Ship Boat Builder.'

South Arm, 1880, prior to the building of the wet dock. All manner of vessels can be seen tied up in the harbour.

Penzance wet dock. The vessel in the foreground is the coaster *Oakford*.

Penzance Harbour, around the turn of the century, showing the extent of the harbour before the ill-advised decision to infill a large proportion of it for parking.

The construction of the wet dock, 1881. This rare photographic print has been taken from a full-plate glass negative in the collection at Penzance Museum.

The Ross Bridge, with the lifeboat house in the background. This bridge was replaced in 1981 after a century of service.

The wet dock gates. It is not known whether this shows the gates prior to their fitting or when they were taken off for maintenance. This picture gives a better impression of the original lifeboat house.

A little accident, 23 July 1930. The Trinity House vessel, TS *Warden*, miscalculated the width of the dock entrance, causing considerable damage to the gates and walls.

Three young lads at Abbey Slip, where one of them has probably been paddling in the inner harbour. This comes from an album of photographs recently purchased by the museum. The photographer is unknown.

Loading china clay. The SS *Spes* was the first ship to load china clay and sail direct to America in 1920. The steam wagons brought the clay from the pits on the St Just road.

Successfully loaded, the vessel leaves Penzance Harbour bound for America.

The *Lyonesse* entering Penzance Harbour. The extreme weather conditions must have made it very difficult for the captain to negotiate the restricted harbour entrance.

Battery Rocks and the sea wall of South Pier. The rigged craft dates this picture to around 1880.

South Pier and lighthouse. The waves breaking over the pier attest to the need for the lighthouse to safeguard vessels .

Ash Wednesday, 1962. Apart from breaking up large sections of the Promenade, the storm washed away huge granite blocks on the south arm of Penzance Harbour.

Batten & Couches Wharf, 1880. Today this is the site of the Jubilee Bathing Pool.

Opening of North Pier, Newlyn, 15 July 1886. Since its construction a further pier has been built out from the centre of the harbour.

Newlyn Harbour. The traditional craft seen here are Mounts Bay Luggers and Pilchard Drivers. The photograph dates from before the completion of North Pier in 1886.

The borough's diver, Omar Pascoe, retained to repair the harbour and sea walls. The pump is preserved in the museum along with the helmet and suit.

Mousehole, from Raginnis Hill, 1908. Tom Bowcocks Eve, a two-hundred-year-old legend, which has been celebrated on 23 December since the 1950s, culminates in the production of Starry-Gazey pie whose ingredients include seven sorts of fish.

Mousehole Harbour, 1891. At this date the harbour was the home of a considerable fishing fleet. Further back in its history, in 1595, the village had been raided by the Spanish, and Squire Jenkin Keigwin was killed.

# Fishing

Newlyn. A fisherman's wife beats (mends) nets outside the front door of her cottage in Newlyn. The pails, bowls, pitchers and bussas indicate that this cobbled yard was the centre of much activity.

Penzance Harbour. The bay is filled with the fishing fleet, the purpose-built Mounts Bay Luggers.

Seine fishing, Mounts Bay. The net boat, with its seine net on board, is probably taking directions from a Huer on the shoreline. This enabled the boat to drop its net right around the pilchard shoal.

Gutting the catch. These three characters are processing a recent catch. The pilchards (fairmaids) were salted down and pressed into barrels, much of the catch being sent to Italy.

Newlyn Old Harbour. This photograph pre-dates the building of North and South Piers. Today this area of Newlyn Harbour is a graveyard for out-of-commission vessels.

Fishwife, 1890. Fish was carried from vessel to market and thence throughout the area by these  ladies with their weatherbeaten faces and cowl, baskets on their backs.

Peeking between the sails of the fishing fleet which has just left the harbour is St Michael's Mount.

These four boys skulling are probably 'whiffing' as well, that is to say fishing with a hook and a piece of string. Skulling is the use of one oar, usually from the back of a small boat.

Billy Renfree, the jowster, or fish-seller, sold his wares throughout Penzance and Newlyn. It is believed that he was a member of the local Jewish community (note his hairstyle).

Two Newlyn fishwives: Betty Lanyon (standing), Blanche Courtney (seated). The unconvincing painted background points to the fact that this is a studio portrait.

Mounts Bay Lugger. Legs were fitted to the sides while in harbour so that the vessel would remain upright whatever the state of the tide

Newlyn Green, 1880. This rare photograph shows nets being put out to dry, possibly after being barked.

The cliff, Newlyn, c. 1890. Until the harbour road was built in 1908, the Newlyn town area and Street an Nowan were only connected when the tide was out.

Until the advent of the plastic kit-box, baskets like these were commonly used for the removal and storage of the catch. This group is outside Sullivan's store, Newlyn.

Staff of the Newlyn Fisheries Exhibition, c. 1890. A number of exhibitions were held at the end of the last century. The Newlyn Fish Festival was relaunched in 1991.

The Old Harbour, Newlyn (pre-1884), with a catch being unloaded. Gibson's photograph has been touched in with the addition of the white line on the lugger in the harbour.

Newlyn Harbour, 1885. This shows South Pier, with North Pier yet to be built.

'An Old Hand', applicable perhaps either to a fisherman or the game of cards in progress.

'French boys.' These young lads obviously hoodwinked 'Flash' Harry Penhaul, as the boy's surname on the extreme right is Downing and at second from right is Harvey.

Lobsters ahoy. The shellfish industry was important in the 1950s but is even more so today. Newlyn Harbour sends its produce throughout Europe and it is a major revenue earner for the district.

Shippams, Newlyn. These ladies seem to have a never-ending supply of pilchards. Once gutted and cooked, these fish were tinned and put on sale in many a high street shop.

# Tourism

'Greetings from Penzance', 25 May 1909. The message on the reverse reads, 'Arrived here safely, having fine time. Lovely weather.' Messages on postcards do not seem to have changed.

The Promenade, 1880. Conflict between fishermen and the hoteliers who wished the beach to be available only for tourists was common between 1860 and 1890. Note the nets put out to dry on the beach.

Bathing machines, c. 1880. The beaches had segregated bathing times so that ladies could use the beach in the morning, the men in the afternoon. A letter in a local newspaper of the time complains that 'women have been spied upon by gentlemen using spy-glasses'!

The Queen's Hotel, which was and still is the premier hotel of the town, has been decorated as part of coronation celebrations, probably in 1902.

QUEEN'S HOTEL,
*Sea-side (on the Esplanade), Penzance.*

The Queen's Hotel. This advertisement is taken from the town's first official guidebook, published by the Corporation in 1876.

The bandstand, 1898. This ornate structure survived until the night of the Ash Wednesday storm in 1962. It was severely damaged and subsequently demolished.

The Promenade, looking east, 1890. The loss of the sand on the beach has always been a problem, as is borne out by the presence of the groynes.

Royal Baths Boarding House and Gibson's studio, pre-1883. The boarding house was famed for its luxury, offering hot and cold baths. Bath night was Saturday, when all the water had to be carried to the bedrooms by hand.

Strolling, just strolling, 1919, the year after the end of the First World War. The structure coming out from the beach was the town's sewage outflow, a problem that is still with us.

Penzance beach, 1927. On the right is the Café Marina and Captain Roger's house. A diving-board off the beach was popular with local youngsters.

Café Marina, 1924. This building catered for all the tourists' needs, whether it was a deck-chair or perhaps afternoon tea accompanied by a stringed orchestra.

The Beachfield, 1924. The monument on the left commemorates the opening of Alexandra Road, and is now in the entrance to the Pirates Rugby Ground.

The Promenade, looking east. The Pavilion had yet to be built and the theatre tent can be seen on its site.

'I do like to be beside the seaside.' Children play on Larriggan rocks in 1927.

This young girl struggling with an inflated inner tube will bring back memories for many a parent.

'Making friends with the gee gee at Penzance.' This title was given to this photograph by Harry Penhaul. He went on to say, 'This genuine snap taken at Penzance in December shows two young ladies making friends with the horse before taking their plunge.'

Jubilee Bathing Pool, just after its completion in 1935. The architect said the design came to him while he watched seagulls alighting on the sea.

The opening of the Jubilee Bathing Pool, 1935. This art deco masterpiece, one of only a few such structures left in this country, is under threat and it is expected to close because of subsidence.

'You too can have a wonderful time!' This publicity photograph, commissioned by Penzance Borough Council from Harry Penhaul, was taken at the Jubilee Bathing Pool.

AERIAL VIEW OF NEW AIRPORT

MAGNIFICENT
CLIFF SCENERY

SHELTERED COVES

TROPICAL GARDENS

MOUNT'S BAY IS
OFTEN CALLED " THE
NAPLES OF
ENGLAND "

ACROSS THE PLACID WATERS OF MOUNT'S BAY TO S

## CORNWALL'S OUTSTANDING HOLIDAY RESORT!

# PENZANCE INVITES YOU *!*

### TO SPEND A GLORIOUS CAREFREE HOLIDAY

THE SENTINEL, MORRAB GARDENS

THE DIVING LESSON

DELIGHTFUL WALKS

MARINE VIEWS

STEAMER TRIPS

TENNIS

BOATING

HUNTING

GOLF

Publicity flier, 1937. This publication publicized the routes to the Isles of Scilly as well as the resort's own amenities.

The humorous postcard, a part of many a seaside holiday. This rather tame example dates from 1907.

Trouble brewing – a holiday trip. A set of six postcards was produced by Gibson, of which three are included in this book. Even at the turn of the century many visitors would go to the Isles of Scilly as part of their holiday.

A first taste of the Atlantic. The crossing to the Isles of Scilly can be very rough.

A general collapse. One wonders whether the crossing was really that bad.

# SECTION EIGHT
# Art and Artists

Artists in Newlyn, 1884. Standing, left to right: Frank Bodilly, Fred Millard, Frank Bramley, Blandford Fletcher, William Breakespeare, Ralph Todd, Alexander Chevallier Tayler, Henry Scott Tuke. Seated: William Wainwright, Edwin Harris, Stanhope Alexander Forbes.

The School of Art, 1880. The school stands alone prior to the building of the Art Gallery.

The Art Gallery. The foundation stone is laid in 1886 by the Mayoress, Mrs Wellington Dale. This is now the main hall of the public library. The gallery was then a part of the School of Art complex.

Walter Langley RBSA was the first artist to arrive in Newlyn who can be associated with the group known today as the Newlyn School.

*In a Cornish Fishing Village; Departure of the Fleet for the North*, 1886, by Walter Langley RBSA. This watercolour is the artist's largest work in this medium and was purchased for the town's art gallery in 1991. The purchase price of £32,400 was raised by public subscription and national grants. In 1886 it sold for 420 guineas.

Stanhope Alexander Forbes RA demonstrating how the artists of the Newlyn School painted *plein air*, i.e. outside. The scene is Boase Street, Newlyn.

The critics. A group of artists assembled on the cliff at Newlyn.

*On Bideford Sands.* This photograph was used by Frank Wright Bordillion to paint the work by the same name which is now in the New South Wales Art Gallery, Sydney, Australia.

Stanhope Alexander Forbes RA in his studio. Many of the well-known Newlyn School paintings were, contrary to popular belief, painted in a studio and not outside.

Elizabeth Adela Forbes, née Armstrong, ARWS. This young Canadian artist came to Newlyn and married Stanhope Forbes in August 1889, following the successful sale to the Tate Gallery of his masterpiece, *The Health of the Bride*.

Norman Garstin. Probably his most famous work is *The Rain it Raineth Every Day*, which he donated to the town in 1889.

Albert Chevallier Tayler and Henry Scott Tuke. These two artists were both members of the Newlyn School. Tuke only stayed in Newlyn a short while before moving to Falmouth.

Percy Craft. Stanhope Forbes did not like this artist's work and suggested that, as he was so successful in staging the amateur dramatic presentations by the artists, he might like to do this instead of painting. Craft went to London and did exactly this.

Inspiration. The Newlyn streets and courts were full of subject material for artists.

Gone fishing. Stanhope Forbes in the centre with two colleagues.

Watching cricket. The artistic communities of Newlyn and St Ives frequently held cricket matches.

The ladies. The mothers, wives and children of the artists after one of the cricket matches.

Amateur dramatics. The members of the Newlyn group of painters held regular amateur dramatic presentations. This could be a rehearsal.

*Plein air*. Percy Craft painting outside. Norman Garstin said, 'Your work cannot really be good unless you have caught a cold doing it.'

Newlyn Art Industries, Champions Slip, Newlyn. J.D. Mackenzie arrived in Newlyn in 1890 and started an art metal class. He was joined in 1892 by John Pearson, a member of the Guild of Handicraft, part of the important Arts and Crafts movement.

Newlyn Copper. The early work of the Newlyn School bore great resemblance to the work of the mainstream Arts and Crafts movement. It was not long, however, before local themes appeared in their work such as fish, birds, luggers and, of course, St Michael's Mount.

Penzance and District Museum and Art Gallery, Penlee House. This was the former home of the Branwells, purchased in 1946 as a war memorial. The building now houses an internationally important collection of paintings and the area's main museum.

# SECTION NINE
# Industry

Wherry Mine, which began working in the early 1700s, was abandoned soon after and restarted in 1798. In 1836 the mine was acquired by a building company, but its operation was short-lived, as it closed in 1838.

Chyandour Smelting House. All ingots of tin produced in these works were stamped with the commonly known 'Lamb and Flat' motif.

Serpentine Works, Wherry Town. Serpentine was popular with the Victorians. Indeed, Queen Victoria ordered a selection for Osborne House, her residence on the Isle of Wight, when she visited Penzance in 1846.

Wharf Road. The quarries from Newlyn to Lamorna supplied stone, including granite, which was used in construction throughout the country. This quarry wagon is on its way to the railway station.

J. Smith's Boot and Shoe Manufactory, Penzance. They obtained the first prize and the first-class diploma for fishermen's boots at the West Cornwall Fisheries Exhibition, Penzance, in 1884.

R.M. Branwell & Sons' flour mill, Gulval. The mill had three steam engines which drove fifteen pairs of grinding stones.

R.M. Branwell & Sons' mill had its own wheelwright's shop and stabling for twenty-four horses. The mill produced one thousand sacks of flour each month. It closed in 1903.

Penlee quarry and Janner's train. This little engine worked between the quarry and the pier at Newlyn. The engine was built in 1901, works no. 73, by Stahlbahnwerke Freudenstien and Company of Templehof, Berlin, Germany.

Hosking's Alexandra Dairy, from the seaward side between the former Bedford Bolitho Gardens and Newlyn Green.

Spring greens. The Mounts Bay area is well known for its mild climate and its excellent agricultural land.

Flower picking. The flower industry has been important to Penwith for nearly one hundred years.

A field of narcissi, *c.* 1890. The flowers are no longer picked in bloom, as today they are preferred in their closed form. The bonnets on the pickers are typical of the costume of country folk of the period.

Harvest time. Threshing day was important to all, and workers from other farms helped. The farmers' wives provided croust which usually included home-produced cider. The portable engine pre-dates the traction engine and would have been moved from farm to farm by horses.

Croust time meant pasties all round and a flask of tea. Croust is the Cornish dialect word for a meal break.

Preparing the ground. These large stones obviously had to be removed before the ground could go under the plough. Many a field in Penwith has needed this treatment.

# Transport

'These newfangled gadgets.' This car has obviously broken down outside the Market House in Penzance and is suffering the indignity of being given a tow by two horses.

Mr Tippet's marvellous machine, 1865. This cycle was built by Mr Tippet, a blacksmith at Kelynack. A later machine also made by him is in the town museum.

E.H. Bostock's menagerie. This wagon pulled by six greys probably held some of Mr Bostock's wild animals.

This wagon with its ornate carvings and elegant paintings would have been the centre-piece of the circus parade. It stands just off the Promenade.

This horse-drawn vehicle was used in Penzance at the turn of the century. The horses would have been dressed with elegant plumes and a man would have walked in front to set the pace for the procession.

This St Just–Penzance horse bus is drawing near to its terminus, the First and Last Inn, at Alverton.

J. Champions & Sons, Jersey car. This service to Logan Rock and Lands End left outside the Mounts Bay Hotel at 9.30 a.m., returning from Lands End at 4 p.m.

This Jersey car going along the Promenade at speed in 1880 was probably also on its way to Lands End. These vehicles met the first 'Down' trains and arrived back in Penzance so that day visitors could catch the last 'Up' train.

J. Champions & Sons, saloon brake. The vehicle is seen outside the Mounts Bay Hotel on the Promenade. The driver is Mr Fred Basset.

The Queen's Hotel carriage. This carriage was used to pick up passengers from the railway station. The driver is the grandfather of Brenda Wotton, the local folk-singer.

The Branwells in front of Penlee House with their carriage and coachman. The stables to the house are now the Penlee Centre, an outpost of Penwith Tertiary College.

Penzance to London. This was the first motor bus service to London, here at Truro.

Motor bus, Penzance station. The Geat Western Railway operated a number of bus services from the station, including those to Margazion and St Just.

Hancock's Sports Arcade. The age of steam on the fairground was coming to an end, *c.* 1920.

The *Elizabeth and Blanche* lifeboat being launched into Penzance Harbour. The boat was removed from Penzance in 1908 and stationed at Newlyn.

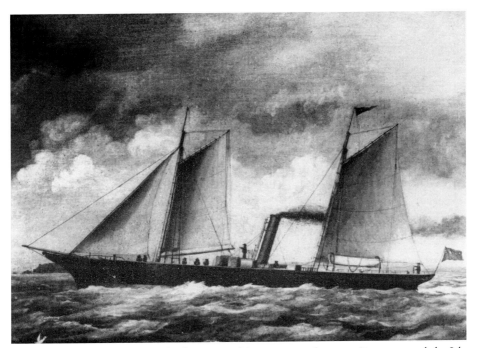

The *Little Western*. This was the first steamship to operate between Penzance and the Isle of Scilly. Operating from 1859, she was wrecked on the islands in 1872.

The *Lyonesse*. Built by Harveys of Hayle, this operated on the Penzance–Isles of Scilly route between 1888 and around 1916.

RMS *Deerhound*. Many vessels have been used to service the Isles of Scilly, including the *Lady of the Isles*, *Lapwing*, *Princess Louise* and the *Queen of the Isles*. The *Deerhound* operated during the early part of the twentieth century.

The *Scillonian*. This was the first purpose-built vessel to be owned by the Isles of Scilly Steamship Company. It was built in Scotland and went into service in 1926.

The *Queen of the Isles*. The Isles of Scilly Steamship Company purchased a second vessel in the 1960s to operate out of Penzance and St Ives. The venture was not successful and the boat was sold.

Penzance railway station, 1870. The railway arrived in Penzance in 1852, but no direct service to London was possible until the Royal Albert Bridge at Saltash was built in 1859. The 7 ft broad guage and the 4 ft 8 in standard guage existed side by side until the week-end of 20–3 May 1892 when all broad-guage rails were lifted and Brunel's grand scheme was finally put to rest.

The Viaduct, Chyandour, prior to the building of the embankment between 1919 and 1921. The engine shed and turntable can be seen in the centre of this picture.

The 'Up' 'Cornish Riviera', London bound, 1 July 1904. The train was initially not named but it was the forerunner of this now famous service.

The 'Down' 'Cornish Riviera', arriving at Penzance on 1 July 1904. The engine was named *Paddington*.

Penzance station, 1912. This colour postcard shows the inside of the station before it was remodelled. The train standing at the platform is a Railmotor, a steam-powered railcar.

'Hall' class locomotive entering Penzance station in August 1945.

Grahame-White and his aeroplane at Trengwainton on 24 September 1913.

Sandy Cove, Newlyn. This was the site of a seaplane base during the First World War.

Channel Air Ferries, Dragon. Air services between the islands and Lands End Aerodrome, St Just, started on 15 September 1937.

Penzance heliport. The Dragon Rapides were replaced by helicopters on 1 May 1964 and services were transferred to Penzance with the opening of the heliport at Penzance by Alfred Beckerleg, Mayor of Penzance, on 1 September 1964.

# Acknowledgements

Thanks are due to the following: Penzance Museum and Art Gallery, and Penzance Town Council; Penzance (subscription) Library, Morrab Gardens and Miss Jan Rhurmund; the Local Studies Library, Redruth; Cornwall County Council and Terry Knight; Dr Eric Richards, stalwart cataloguer of the museum's photographic collection who made this book possible; Felicity Richards for the computerization of the initial catalogue; Rosemary Dennis for proof reading; Elizabeth Brock for sorting and refiling the chosen photographs; Carole, my wife, who has had to put up with a mountain of photographs in our dining-room; last, but not least the photographers themselves, Robert Preston, Gibson, Moody, Harry Penhaul, Richards, Frith, Valentine, Paul Brothers, and the many others who unfortunately did not put their name to their work.